RETFORD

OLD AND NEW

A NEW TAKE OF SOME OLD VIEWS OF RETFORD

RON BEARE

Published by
REDI-IMAGE.COM
ONLINE TO THE BEST PICTURES

Sycamore House, Sutton cum Lound.
Retford, Nottinghamshire. DN22 8QB

ISBN 978-0-9556158-0-1

FIRST EDITION 2007

Copyright © Ron Beare

All rights reserved, no part of this edition may be reproduced, stored in a retrieval system or transmitted in any form or by any means electronic, mechanical, photocopying, recording, or otherwise, without the prior written permission of the publisher and copyright owner.

Printed by
Bayliss Printing Company Ltd
Shireoaks Triangle, Worksop. S81 8AP

Acknowledgements

I am deeply indebted to the following for their valuable assistance in the production of this book

To the late Percy Laws and Eric Smith, without their help and encouragement in
my early photographic years, this project would never have even been started.

To the numerous audiences of the "Retford Old and New" slide show, who over the last
two decades have insisted that it would make an excellent book. Your patience is rewarded.

To the kind people who have always been willing to loan me me their treasured
original pictures, enabling me to "do a quick copy" for my archives.
In particular Peter Dixon and Albert Phillipson for allowing access to
their collections of images of the town and surrounding areas.

To the photographers who had the forsight to record images of Retford for posterity.
Your copyright is acknowledged and respected. I trust that you agree with my
sentiments that these images should be made available for everyone's
enjoyment and not left forgotton, covered in dust, in some drawers.
Now we can show everyone the Retford we knew.

Last but not least, the Staff of The Bassetlaw Museum,
for being a constant source of encouragement and information, thank you

This journal makes no pretence of being a pictorial history of Retford.
It doesn't purport to make any statement as to whether
or not the town may have improved or perhaps deteriorated
a little during the past one hundred years.

The photographic comparisons are presented side by side,
in black and white for you to form your own conclusions,
with a few anecdotes thrown in to help revive a memory or two.

If you're new to the area, please follow the book's trail around
the town, noting as you go how Retford has changed,
see what it once contained, the good and not so perfect.
Use caution as the route passes many hostelries,
even a half in each may be considered excessive!

If you are an Old Retfordian in exile, you can enjoy the nostalgia for the
things that we once knew. Feel free to take that trip down memory lane,
then look to see what's happened in your absence.

ENJOY!

THE TOUR AROUND TOWN

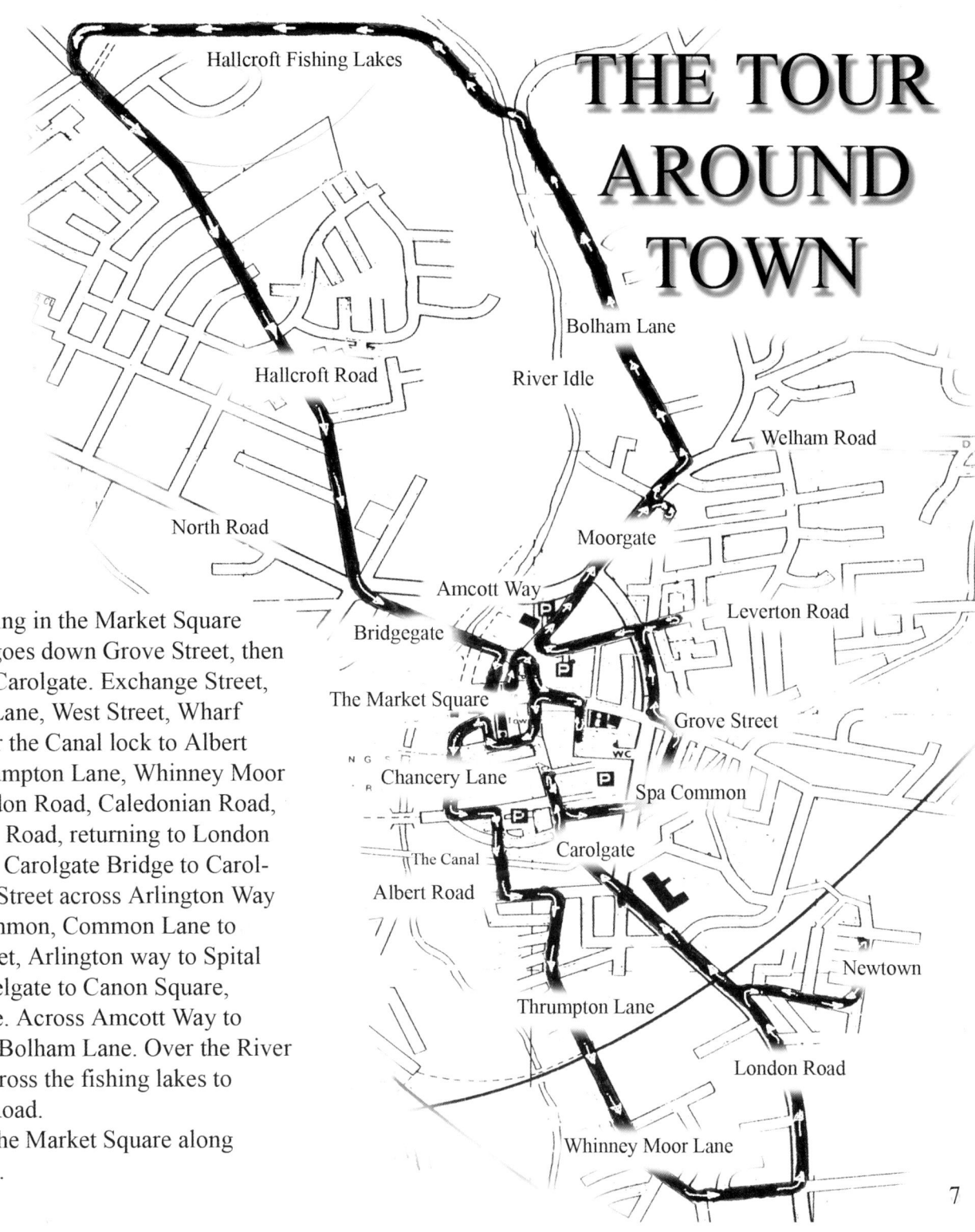

Starting in the Market Square The route goes down Grove Street, then back onto Carolgate. Exchange Street, Chancery Lane, West Street, Wharf Road. Over the Canal lock to Albert Road, Thrumpton Lane, Whinney Moor Lane, London Road, Caledonian Road, Strawberry Road, returning to London Road. over Carolgate Bridge to Carolgate, New Street across Arlington Way to Spa Common, Common Lane to Grove Street, Arlington way to Spital Hill, Chapelgate to Canon Square, Churchgate. Across Amcott Way to Moorgate, Bolham Lane. Over the River Idle and across the fishing lakes to Hallcroft Road.
Return to the Market Square along Bridgegate.

The Market Square, North Side.

No major reconstruction here, but some facade modifications. The Social Security building had two huge windows put in and became Sinclair's, then later Stanley Hunt Jewellers.
The Retford Savings Bank and Smith Fosters Wine Merchants all evolved into Lloyds TSB's premises. The Needlecraft and Wool Shop amalgamated into the Yorkshire Bank premises. The financial company who took over the North Notts Farmer's shop made an excellent job of removing all the paintwork, exposing the fine old Georgian brickwork frontage.

White Hart Corner, The Market Square

Not a lot of building changes here over the past sixty years, only the occupants. Goodsons became Timothy Taylor's fruit shop for a few years; followed by a succession of tennants. Connoisseur jewellers replaced Curry's bicycles who moved into Carolgate with a whole new range of items for sale. Fred Spencer moved into Sargentsons, selling gents outfits. I seem to remember wearing a similar cap to the schoolboys when I went to Sir Frederick Milner School in the 50's.

The Market Square, North East Side. '60's

B.R.Neale and Wright Bro's shops have been aquired to make way for one of the town's first supermarkets. The premises later being occupied by Argos.
Baker Bro's little Cannon Cafe had also closed when this shot was taken, later Bernard Gould opened as a gents outfitter.

Rowell's Corner. The Market Square

Some major structural changes here. As well as Wrights and Neale's shops being replaced, the old gas board and Pollards of Perth premises were demolished to make way for the new gas board showrooms.
Rowell's clothiers shop had a strange aerial contraption that propelled little containers of money to the accounts office, returning with the change and a reciept.

11

The Market Square, The East side

This row of shops included Wildbores, upholsterers; Hodson and Hardman, printers; Boots the Chemist; Segars clothing shop; Howards Cafe, on three floors. We always had to go up to the top floor for tea on a Saturday, this gave a great view when the fair was on the square and it was getting dark. I think the shop on the corner at this time was the Home and Colonial Stores.

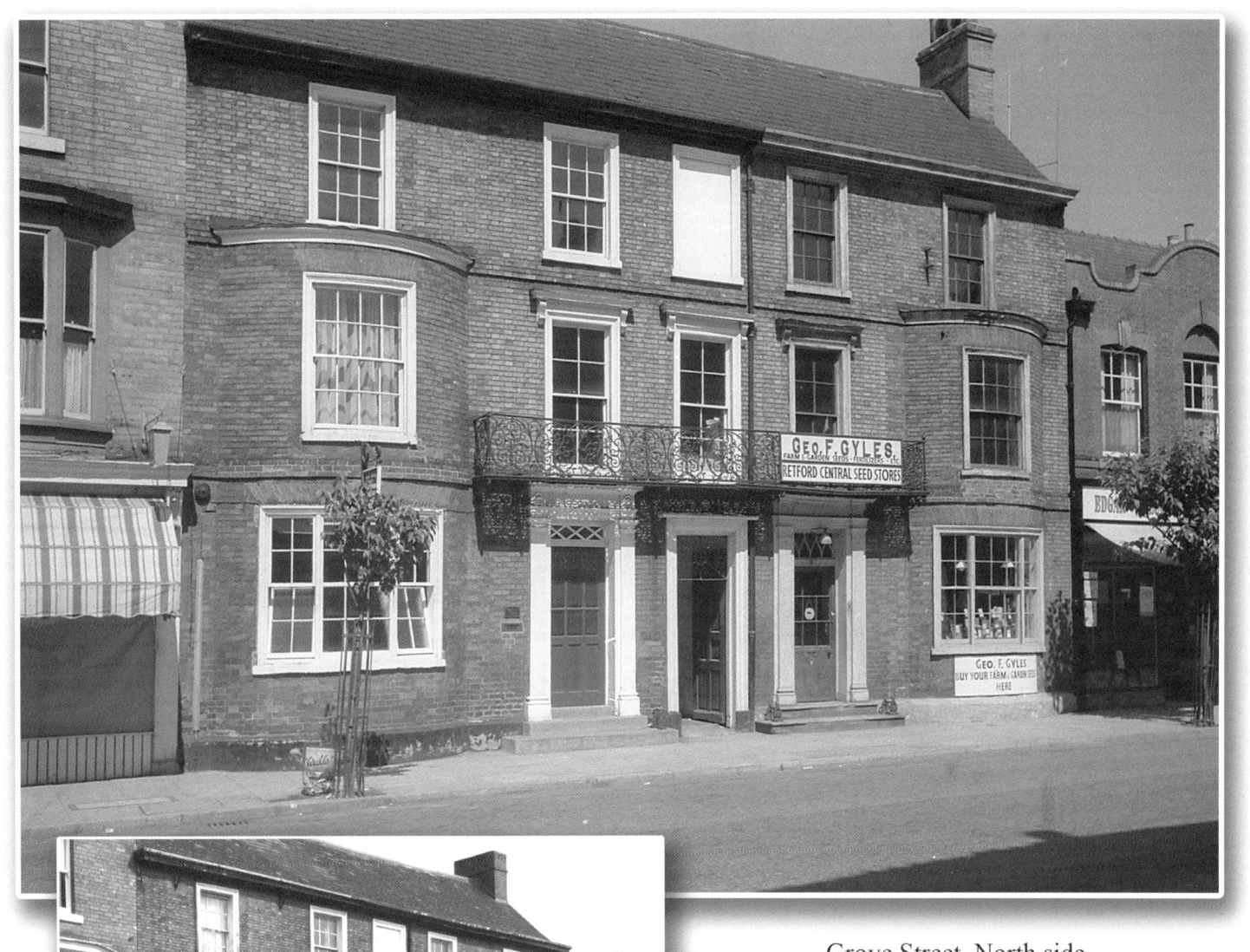

Grove Street, North side

Next to the sweet shop was Selby's Cycle shop. I got my Capri scooter from there. Ray Butler gave me my first lesson on Grove Street, there weren't many cars on the street in the early 'sixties! The premises next to Geo F Gyles is now Britalia Coffee Shop. Edgar Welchman's were the town's longest established photographers. Percy Laws worked for them before opening his own studio on Carolgate Bridge.

Grove Street, Beardsall's Row

This row of houses disappeared when the road was widened for the bus station. On the right can be seen the roofs of the Grove Street Methodist Chapel, Amcott House and Bingham's Central Garage. At the far end of Beardsall's Row, on Grove Street, was Retford's first Co-op shop. On the opposite side of Grove Street, Mr Harworth had his dental surgery

The Market Square, Grove Street Corner

Fletcher's were a large outfitters shop with sales departments on more than one floor. Just as in Rowell's shop they had a contraption that shot little containers of money to and from their accounts department.
The Granby Hotel was next door on Carolgate.
It's very difficult to believe that the main road from London to Edinborough went past this spot in those days; see the A1 sign in front of the shop.

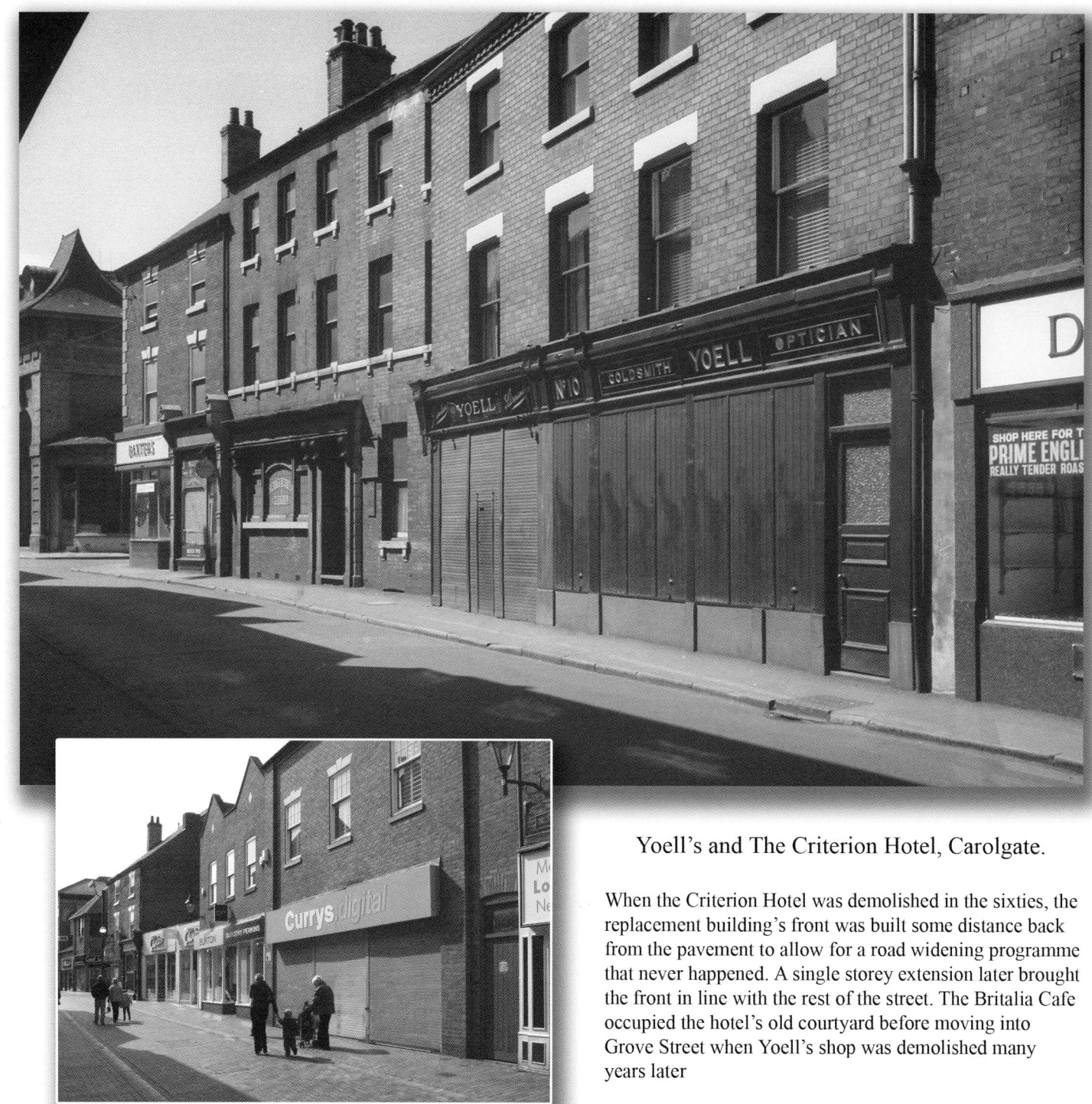

Yoell's and The Criterion Hotel, Carolgate.

When the Criterion Hotel was demolished in the sixties, the replacement building's front was built some distance back from the pavement to allow for a road widening programme that never happened. A single storey extension later brought the front in line with the rest of the street. The Britalia Cafe occupied the hotel's old courtyard before moving into Grove Street when Yoell's shop was demolished many years later

The Shambles and Curtis and Howell Ltd

The Shambles was an indoor meat market with stalls.
Sam Adam's had the greengrocery shop on the corner of Exchange Street.
Curtis and Howell were one of the largest ironmongery stores in the district and had daily deliveries out into the surrounding area.

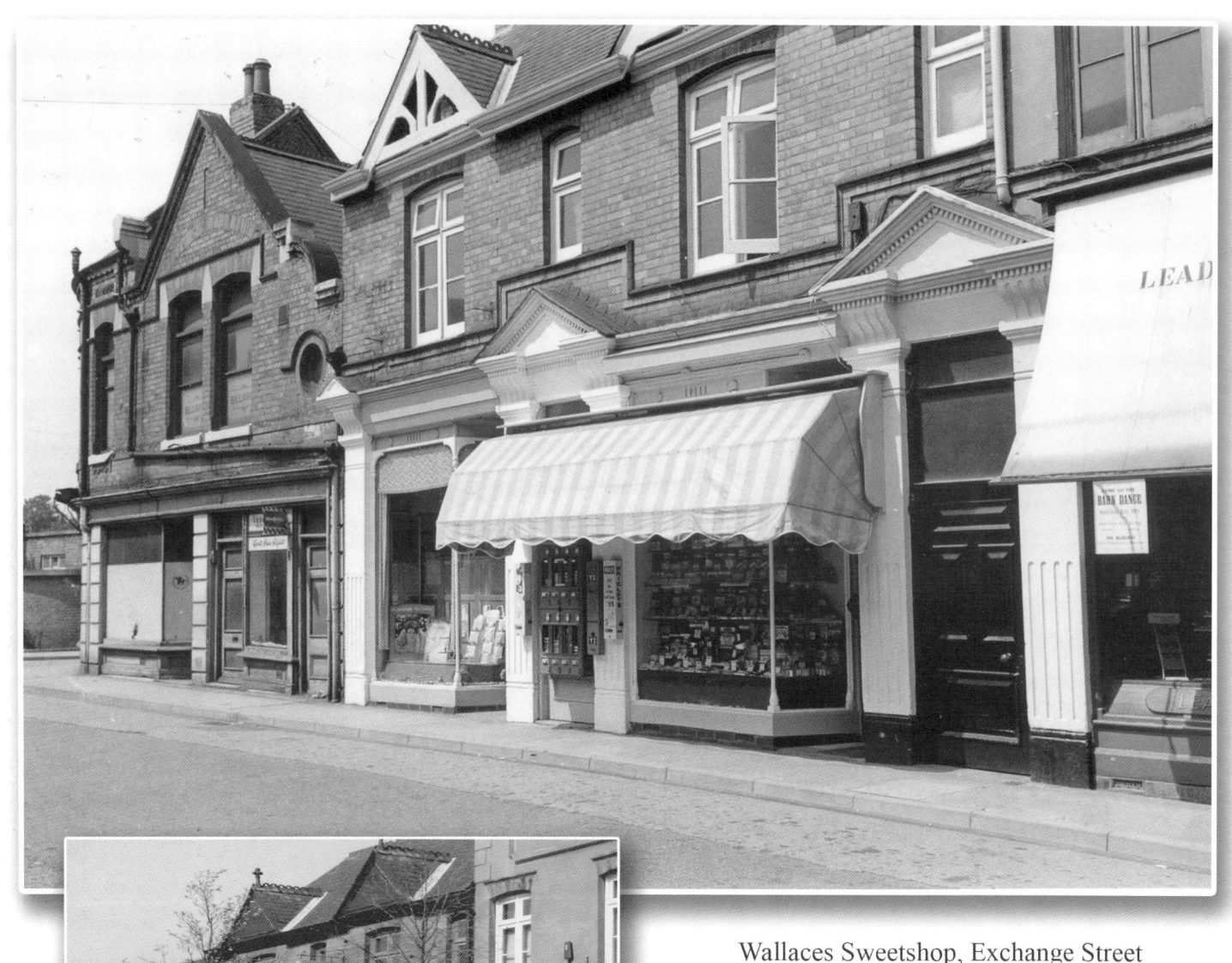

Wallaces Sweetshop, Exchange Street

Wallace's sweetshop moved from the corner to next door to Ivy Basher's ladies shop, later both premises were amalgamated to become Papa's fish and chips. It's doubtful if cigarette vending machines could be positioned outside any shop these days!
The poster advertises a barn dance on July 18th at Field Farm, East Drayton, dancing to The Blue Jays. I can clearly remember that evening, but we wont go into the reason why.

The Criterion Billiard Rooms, Exchange Street

Beneath the Criterion Hotel's billiard rooms were Faulkners turf accountant's and Pete Mellor's gents hair stylist shops. Ivy Basher's ladies shop and Milner and Lazenby's coal merchant's office were next, along with Leadbeater and Peters the Optician's. Baxters the Butchers on the corner had another shop on Bridgegate.

Town Hall Yard, Exchange Street

The Retford Paper Bag shop is just out of sight down the yard.
Between Wilf Faulkner's watch repair shop and Wallace's sweet shop was the rear entrance to the Criterion Hotel. Above Wallace's and the betting shop next door was the hotel's billiard room. Wallaces sweetshop was always a stop off on the way to the pictures, the sweets were always cheaper there.

Chancery Lane, The Fur and Feather Market

In the courtyard behind this long building, the rabbits and poultry used to be sold. It was also home to the infamous "Smokey Joes" cafe, somewhere we as youngsters were forbidden to go into. By the time I was old enough to know the reason why, it had closed!
Chambers shop on the end was, I am told, either a gun-shop or a travel agents, not a lot of difference.

21

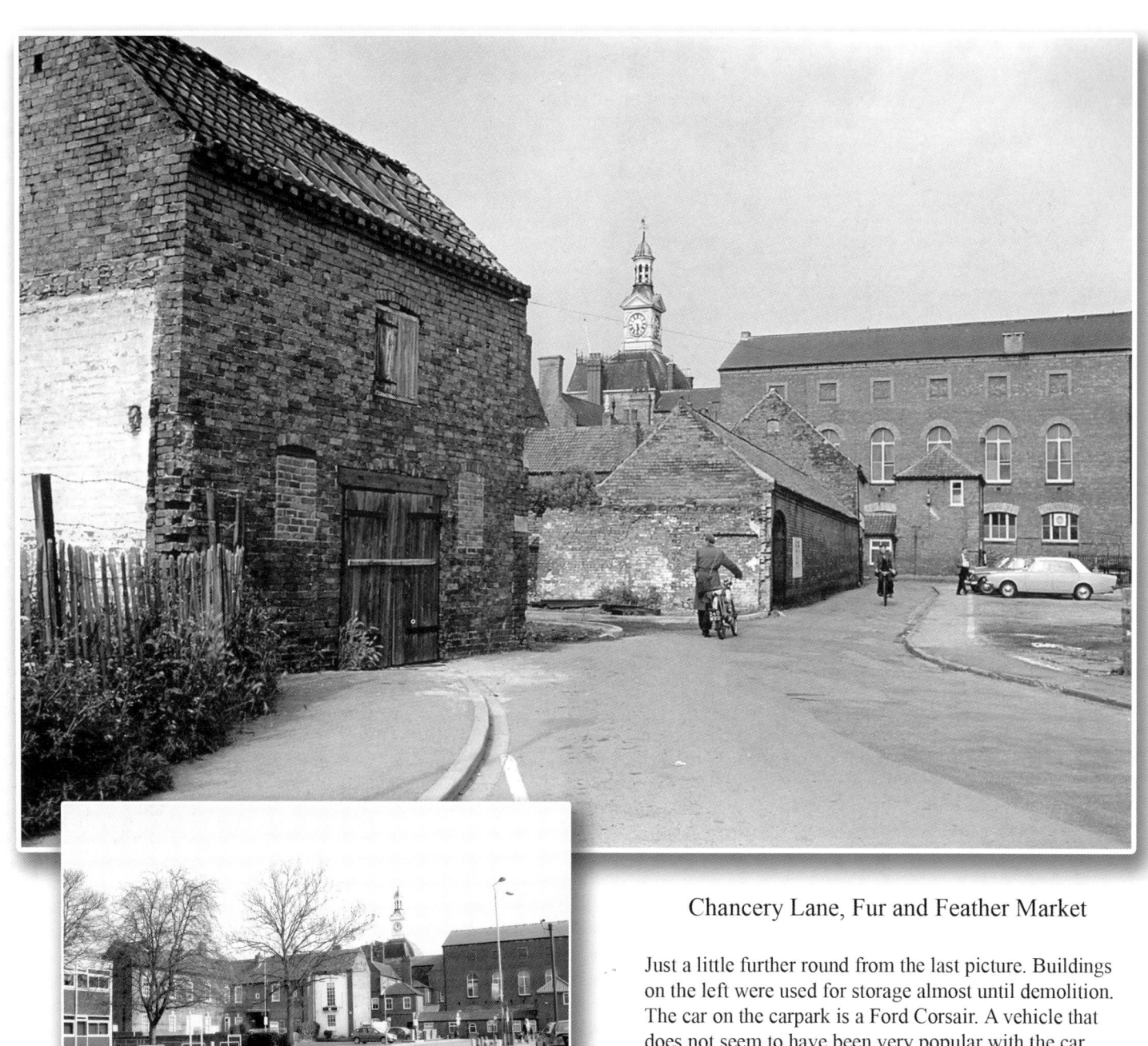

Chancery Lane, Fur and Feather Market

Just a little further round from the last picture. Buildings on the left were used for storage almost until demolition. The car on the carpark is a Ford Corsair. A vehicle that does not seem to have been very popular with the car preservation people, possibly because they were very prone to rusting.

Chancery Lane, The Fur and Feather Market

In amonst this jumble of buildings, Jim Preston had his ice cream business. Part of one of his vehicles can be seen on the right hand side.
When everything was finally demolished the ice cream business relocated to Frederick Street. Dr Parry had his surgery in the large building and Daff's the straw merchant used part of the same premises as offices.

West Street, Hope Terrace, The Carr

This row of houses looked out onto the children's playing field at the side of Kings Park. There we played for hours on equipment that is now considered to be far too dangerous for todays children.
Beyond the bay windowed houses in the distance was Richmond's builders yard. Over Carr bridge, going over the River Idle, was what we always knew as the celery fields, I dont recall ever seeing any celery growing there though.

West Street, Pickerings Shop

Right accross the road from the old Retford Times printing works on the corner of Chancery Lane. For many years the site was used as a car park and dumping ground before the Carolgate service road was completed.
The old enamel signs for Watson's Matchless Cleanser, Hudson's Soap and Rowntree's Cocoa would be worth something to today's memorabilia collectors.

West Street, Japanese Terrace

I have not been able to find out how this row of houses came to be so named.
Before the inner ring road came through there was an unbroken row of houses right down to the Carr bridge. The far end properties were very prone to flooding.

Spring Gardens to The Carr, West Street.

These houses, opposite The White Lion public house were demolished in the 'sixties and, until quite recently the land remained undeveloped or was just being used as rough carparking. The Retford Times relocated here from the end of Chancery Lane, their old premises demolished and replaced with new office accomodation.

West Street, Rear of The White Lion Pub

I have heard this called slaughterhouse lane but cant confirm it. Eddie Green the fishmonger had his fish store in the brick building on the extreme right of the old picture.

West Street, Thacker's Bakery

Two bakeries operated almost side by side, Bamforth's and Thacker's. Mr Thacker could be seen delivering bread around the local villages, usually with a large wicker basket and wearing a pair of leather gaiters over his trousers. The shop became a tv repair business, then a plant hire company and is currently an opticians.

J W Knight's Tyres & Richmond's yard, West Street.

John Knight set up his first tyre depot here shortly after leaving Clarks Tyres. To one side of him Cedric Shaw repaired radios and televisions, whilst on the other, Richmond and Sons Ltd, had a large timber storage yard.
The building with the three short chimney's, visable above the timber yard is the Roxy Cinema, demolished in the seventies.

West Street, Haslam Square

A square of houses with a common courtyard in the centre. I was told in the 1970's that some of the landlords could not be traced, so much needed repair work could not be carried out. The only option was rehousing the occupants and demolishing the buildings. Richmond's timber yard became another car park, whilst Pickle's newspaper distribution centre went on to be a pre- school playgroups premises.

The Broken Wheel Disco, Wharf Road.

Originally a canalside warehouse, built in the 18th century to store goods brought up by boat on the adjacent waterway. During the swinging sixties it was the venue for seeing some great acts. the poster on the wall advertises "Jimmy James and The Vagabonds" and "Ben E King"
Later the home of Discount Cycles, it's now awaiting a scheme of renovation.

Wharf Road, The Corporation Lock

The first of the narrow locks that prevented larger vessels from proceeding further inland. Goods had to be offloaded onto smaller boats and fees paid at the canal office next to the lock-keeper's cottage. The fire station tower with air raid siren can be seen in the distance, to the left of the Congregational Chapel, recently replaced by a new supermarket.

Spicers Board Mills, Albert Road.

Opened in 1867 and, because of its close proximity to the railway, putting Bolham Paper Mill out of business. When this photograph was taken almost a hundred years later, the Company was still expanding. Forty years, and a few new owners later, the only thing left to remind us of what was once there is the Mill Bridge Close name.

Thrumpton Lane, The Rifleman's Arms

Most probably named after the Sherwood Regiment, now has the much less posh name of Ma Hubbard's. This would have been a very handy hostelry for Northern Rubber and Jenkin's workers when their shift finished.

Jim Preston's ice cream business moved onto nearby Frederick Street when his old premises on Chancery Lane were listed for demolition.

Thrumpton Lane, W J Jenkin's rear entrance

The back way into the large engineering works. The wires going to the chimney aren't for the telephones, but belonged to the Radio Relay Company who operated from premises on Carolgate. They broadcast radio programmes via the wires to a loudspeaker in the home. Channel choice was very limited. The little fellow running to the sweetshop could be possibly be Andrew Paul.

Whinney Moor Lane, Feeder Cottages

Close to these cottages ran the feeder, a stream diverted from the River Idle to eventually feed water into the Chesterfield Canal near Osberton Road, off Dominie Cross Road.
Behind the tree on the right can be seen the end wall of the now demolished Thrumpton Infant's School.

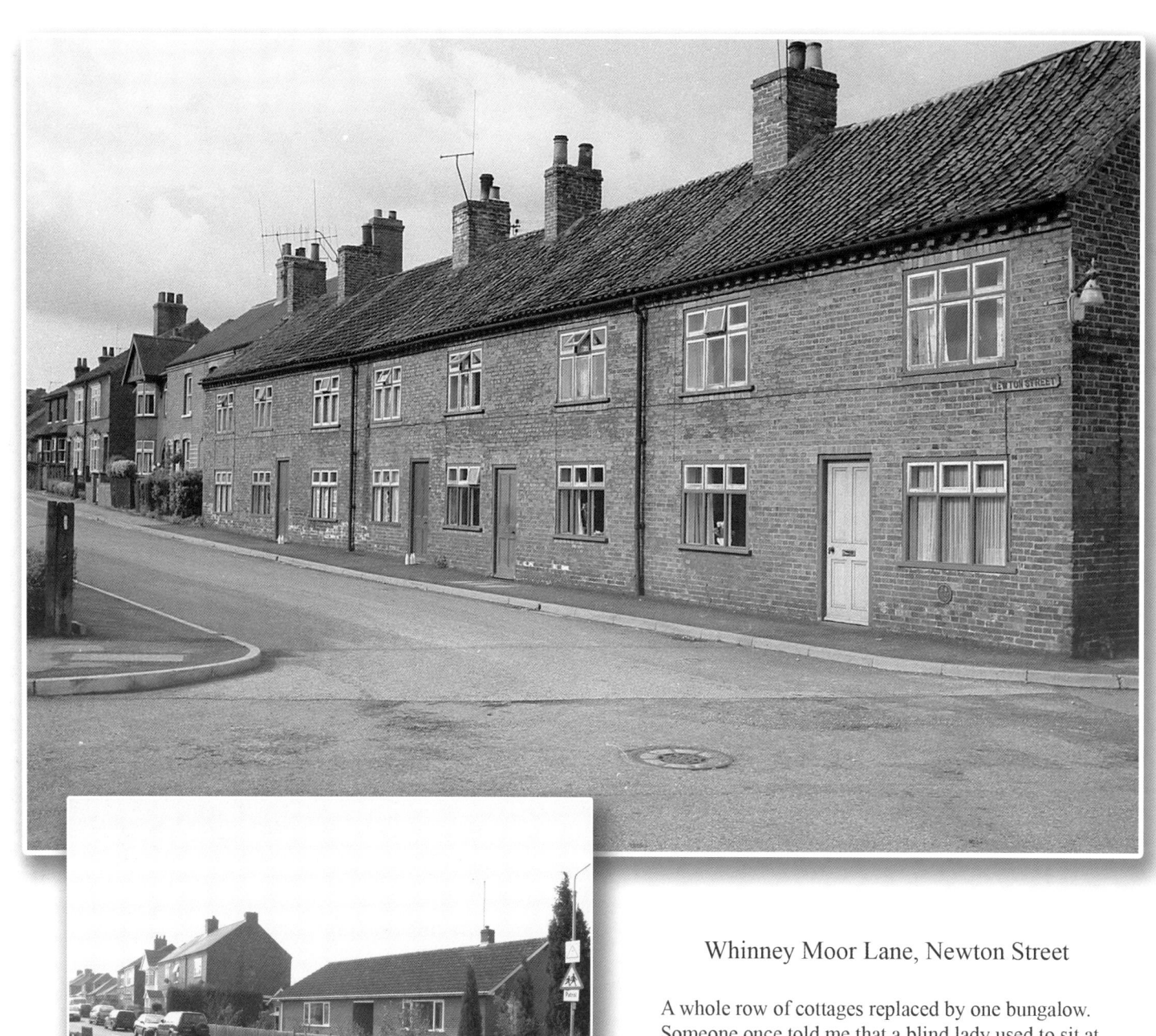

Whinney Moor Lane, Newton Street

A whole row of cottages replaced by one bungalow. Someone once told me that a blind lady used to sit at the end window looking out. Now I wonder how she managed to do that?

London Road and Whinney Moor Lane.

I often wondered why this little row of cottages had storm shutters on the downstairs windows.
Was it perhaps to prevent drunks from accidentally breaking a window on their way home from nearby hostelry's The Elms and The Nags Head?
Documents dating back to the time of Queen Anne were found during the demolition of the buildings.

London Road, Inkerman's Flats

When the original photograph was taken in the '60's, the flats were in imminent threat of demolition.
A developer renovated the building creating individual apartments for sale.
Dawn Cragg later converted the property at the southern end into the South Lawns guest house.

Caledonian Road, Newtown.

The entrance to Newtown from London Road.
The narrow gap at the end of the row of houses used to lead to Wilson's mill, demolished in 1937.
Interestingly, Mr Davidson's corrogated iron shed still survives after nearly fifty years.

Cross Street, off Strawberry Road, Newtown.

An unadopted street until the early 1970's, when it was tarmaced and kerbed. The tall poplar trees were a Retford landmark, now only a couple remain standing.
The backs of Wharton Street houses can be seen in the distance. An alleyway led through to the street and was a favourite spot for courting couples.

Strawberry Road, Newtown

These houses, made with bricks from the brickyard just accross the road were defiled when the town went through a period of stone cladding fever in the 70's and 80's. One Councillor, Chris Fawcett vehemently opposed the practice, but failed to stop many properties being refaced with the coloured concrete tiles.

Hind Street, off Strawberry Road, Newtown.

Mrs Flinton looks over the hedge, that little dog used to have a go at anybody walking down the street.
Peter Johnson's little Austin Seven sportster on the left, eventually went off to the scrapyard, today the car would be a collectors item.
The street was paved and parking bays provided as part of the Newtown improvement scheme in the early 1970's.

Hodgson's Car Showroom, London Road

Herbert Hodgson bought a large area of land at the end of South Street and London Road to create a large Ford Main Dealership. The business has changed hands a few times since Hodgson's departure in the mid eighties.

I'm afraid I'm responsible for the vandalism on the house! A group of us who worked for Hodgson's helped to demolish the properties. Everything that could be recycled was saved and reused, including all the roof tiles.

The Railway Inn, London Road.

Popularly known as "The Ranch", possibly because of the long bar in the main room, although some say it was because one particular landlord had a habit of wearing a stetson hat.

46

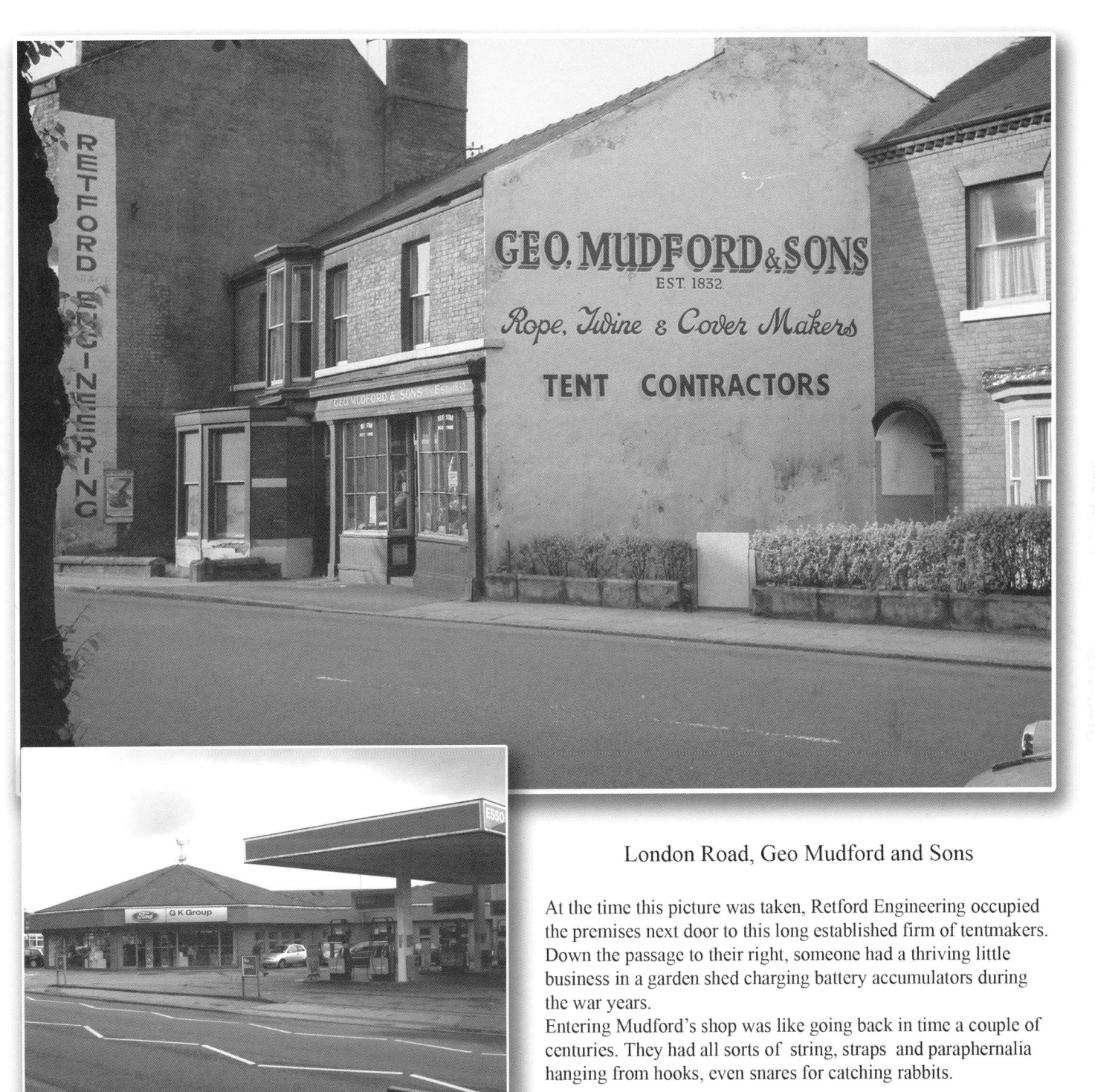

London Road, Geo Mudford and Sons

At the time this picture was taken, Retford Engineering occupied the premises next door to this long established firm of tentmakers. Down the passage to their right, someone had a thriving little business in a garden shed charging battery accumulators during the war years.

Entering Mudford's shop was like going back in time a couple of centuries. They had all sorts of string, straps and paraphernalia hanging from hooks, even snares for catching rabbits.

London Road, Mudford and Sons

Taken shortly after the "disaster". For weeks we had been very carefully demolishing the buildings next door in our spare time in preparation for Hodgson's new filling station and car showroom to be built on the site.

The front wall was deemed unsafe for us to demolish as there was the possibility of it falling across the London Road, so a "professional" demolition team was employed to do the work safely. Unfortunately they got it all wrong and the main road was closed for half a day whilst they cleared up the debris

London Road Post Office.

At the side of the Post Office, Alex Burgess had his butchers shop, later to be taken over by John Wass. Further along was Bradley's green grocery shop. All were long established businesses. When the greengrocer's shop was demolished Mr Bradley moved to a new shop on Rufford Avenue, Ordsall. Trading conditions in this area are severely restricted by the traffic conditions and no business currently seems to survive for more than a few months.

London Road and Wright Wilson Street

Why Shell Cottage is so ornately decorated is unclear, perhaps it was because the owner worked for the local stonemason who had a little gravestone display in the yard.
When I was youngster, I used to walk along the top of the wall. I could never understand why someone would have people buried in their garden.

London Road, Thurman's

A price tag on a ladies slip in the window says 11/6, the princely sum of 58p in todays decimal currency. Dorothy's sweet shop was always popular with the boys from the Grammar School accross the road.

51

Gladish's Corner, Carolgate Bridge.

On the left hand side was Gladish's grocery shop, later to become Kingston's, then Bingham's Carpets before being demolished to make way for the ring road. Further up the bridge were Darwin's newsagents, Clark's the Cleaners, Hodgson's Regent garage and Robert Burns the Chemist. On the other side of the road, The Palace Cinema became Rodway's Garage before being rebuilt as the Ritz cinema and finally becoming the Masonic Hall.

Carolgate, Calamite House and Dominie Cross

THE RINK, refers to The Olympia skating rink, an indoor roller skating rink at the side of the canal.
 The trees hide Mr Brough the Dentist's house and Dominie Cross Road. This is reputed to be the original site of the town's Broadstone, now in the market square.
Properties further along London Road have over the years housed Vicker's the Bakers and Selby's cycle shop.

Carolgate Bridge.

This once thriving row of business's faded away in the early 80's when the ring road opened.
My photographic studio was next door to Bingham's Carpets, above them on the first floor, the Cats Cradle Nightclub. Others over the years have included The Handymans shop; Jackson's, Geoffrey, and Wilf Parker, all hairdressers; a Tailor, Mr Brown; Peter Ward's TV's; Radio Relay; Trent Hire and right at the top near the canal, "shoddy" Shaw the Cobbler.

Carolgate Bridge, The Anchor Corner

The building in the centre once housed the Radio Relay shop. In the back room a large radio and amplifier system sent radio programmes all over town via a network of cables strung from property to property. A simple rotary switch on a loudspeaker box provided the "channel" tuning.

Brewery lane at the side lead down to The Retford Brewery, this later became a fertiliser works before Smiths Flour Mills moved onto the site.

57

Carolgate, Willows Gents Outfitters

Willows occupied a large shop next to Curtis and Howell the ironmongers before "downsizing" to premises on the corner of Exchange Street and The Town Hall yard. Bowskills and Freemans were both newsagents on opposite sides of Carolgate.

Carolgate, Glasby's Grocers Shop

The strongest memory that folks had about Glasby's was the wonderful aroma of freshly ground coffee. This was prepared using a hand turned machine with a large brass wheel on it, discharging the coffee grounds into a little brown paper bag.
Georgian House to the right was once The White Swan public house, with stabling through an archway into it's rear courtyard.

Glasby's and Arlington House, New Street.

Beyond the rear entrance to Glasby's can be seen the top of Arlington House. Originally a private residence, it later became a fever hospital, saw service during the war as a firewatch base; the tall tower on the roof is a lookout post. Finally ending its days as a warehouse for Oates the builder's merchants.

New Street, The Wharf

To the left hand side of these cottages was once a large basin joined to the canal, hence the wharf connection. To the right can be seen what remained of the Retford and Worksop Brewery, the slatted roof vents to let the steam out.
The pipework above was part of Smiiths Flour Mills which used to be down Brewery Lane, off Carolgate where the new supermarket is.

New Street, Sharpe Stone Mason.

Behind the stonemason's yard can be seen Arlington House, which during its lifetime has been a private house, a fever hospital, during WW2 it was a firewatch position; the tower on the roof was a lookout post. Its final use before demolition was Oates Builders Merchants sales and store.

New Street, The Labour Hall

Why so many bricked up windows? The three storey section had to be demolished because it was unstable.
Quite close to here was Henderson Hall, lost under the Co-op extensions and car park.

The Ivy Leaf Social Club, Spa Common.

The little wooden hut sandwiched between the houses provided drink and entertainment. Two new venues appeared after it was demolished, the Labour Hall on New Street and the Bridge Centre accross the ring road on Spa Common.

Kirke and Bescoby Streets, off Spa Common.

Harold Cutts and Mervyn Clark had builder's businesses on Spa Common. The houses on Kirke and Bescoby Street were all replaced by modern flats. Bob Lockwood's potato lorry makes a delivery on the common, site of the sheep fair. Retford's remaining gasholder is just visible above the white building in the centre of the picture.

Grove Street, The St Swithun's School

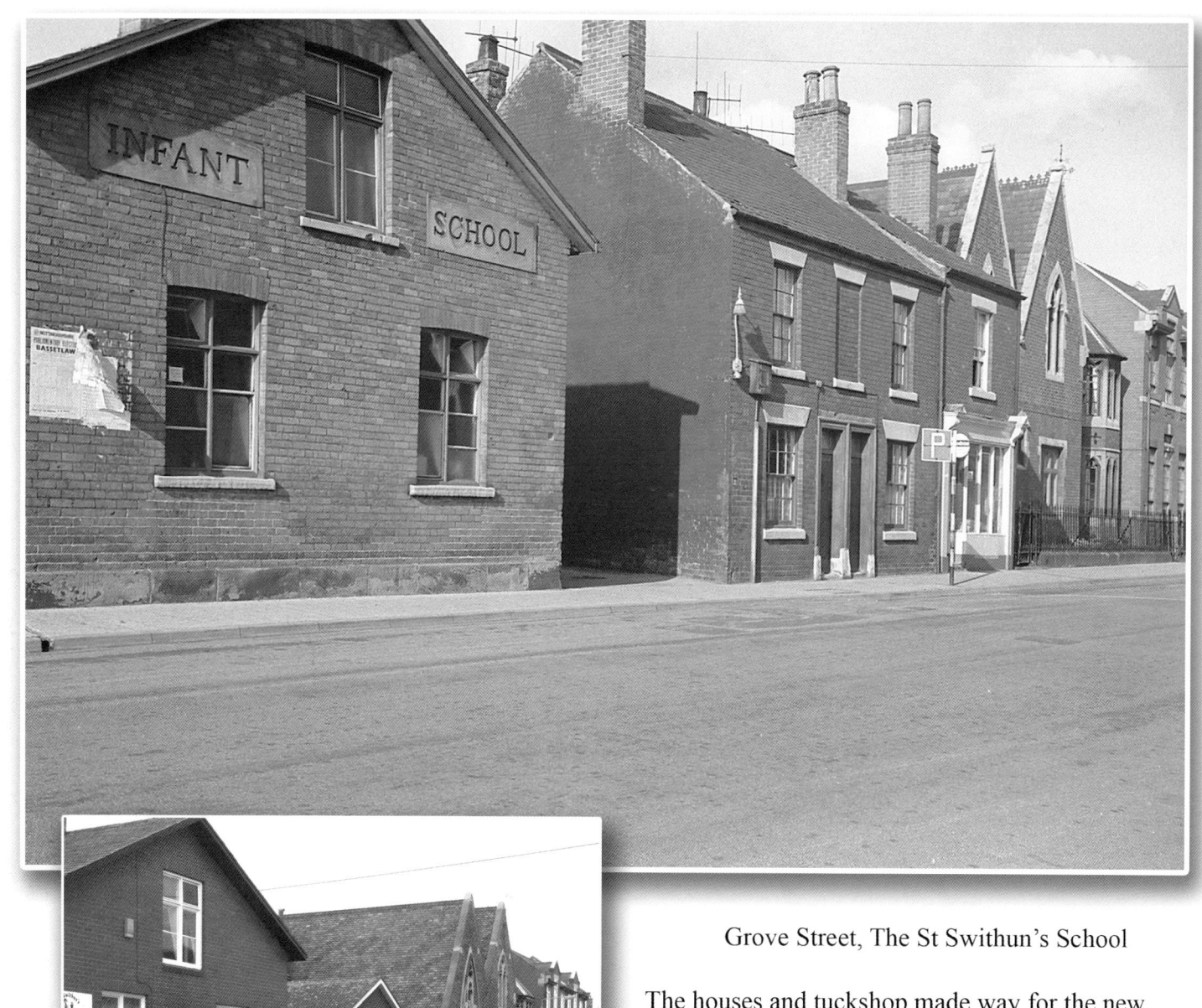

The houses and tuckshop made way for the new dining hall, whilst the end wall of the infant school had to be replaced because of structural problems. Replacement windows almost match the originals, but they failed to put back into position the stone " INFANT SCHOOL" names.

Grove Street, The Wesleyan Chapel

Now on the busy junction with the ring road, once only Union Street passed by the Chapel's other side. Photographing a wedding party on the front steps was easy as very little traffic came down Grove Street.

The tall chimney is part of Clark's Dyeworks, which used to be in what is now Dyer's Court in Chapelgate car park.

Spital Hill, Birkett's Shop

Was he an inspiration for Ronnie Barker's " Open all hours"? Probably so.

Almost every essential for the home could be purchased here, note the brush stand on the pavement. It's doubtful if the wall mounted cigarette vending machine would last long in this area now.

Currie's had a fish and chip shop in the front room of the last house on the right, later moving to newly built premises just a few yards down the hill,

Chapelgate, The Cannon Square

The Crown Hotel was the headquarters of the Retford Motor Club for many years. Further along the street Billy Bowskill sold fireworks and had a childrens play area at the rear of the shop. In the distance can be seen the Chapel at the end of Union Street, which was used by Blyth Model Dairies as an egg processing plant.

Churchgate, St Swithun's Church

No up to date picture here, little has changed over the centuries.

Churchgate, The Cannon Square

Just a little further along from The Vine Inn was the Registrar's Office. After the civil ceremony we used to cheat and take the wedding party accross the road into St Swithun's churchyard for the photographs.

I was once told that it was pure coincidence that the cannon is in exact alignment with the tax office on Bridgegate.

The tax office has since moved accross the road, so maybe the thing should be moved around a little?

Churchgate

Things changed drastically on Churchgate when the ringroad turned it literally into a dead end street. Moorgate started at the premises immediately behind the horse and cart. Leaded windows in the leather shop on the right hand side remain, despite the fact that there have been two world wars since this photograph was taken.

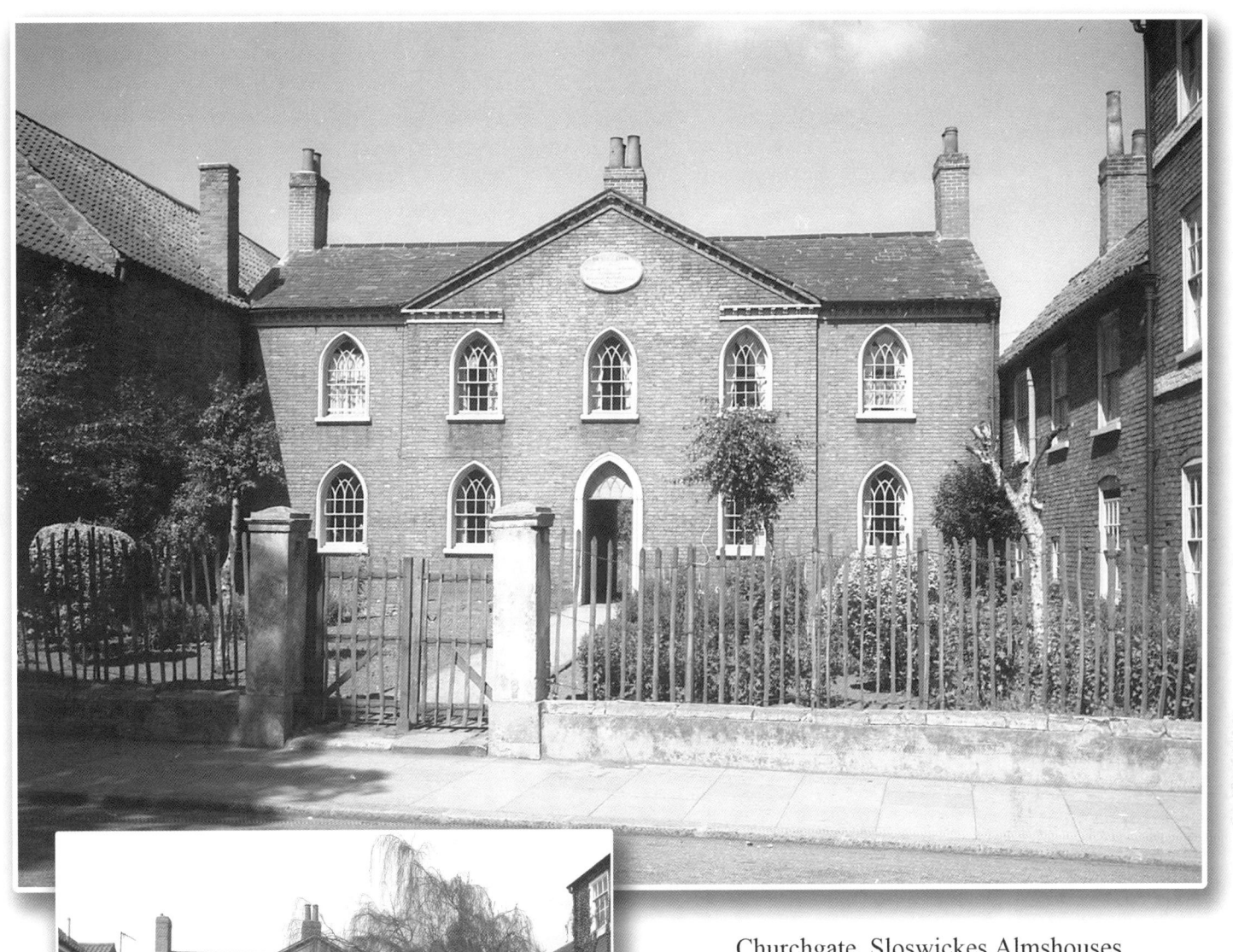

Churchgate, Sloswickes Almshouses

Not a lot of change here. Tim Taylor's fruit shop and building to the left of the almshouses has gone, making way for an new extension. The chestnut fencing has been replaced with iron railings and the silver birch tree still survives after over forty years of pruning.

Churchgate

Dr Mackrill had his surgery through the first archway and a few years later Kath Straker MBE opened Pinewood House catering shop in the last premises before the Churchgate car park. When this picture was taken, the car park area would still be gardens.

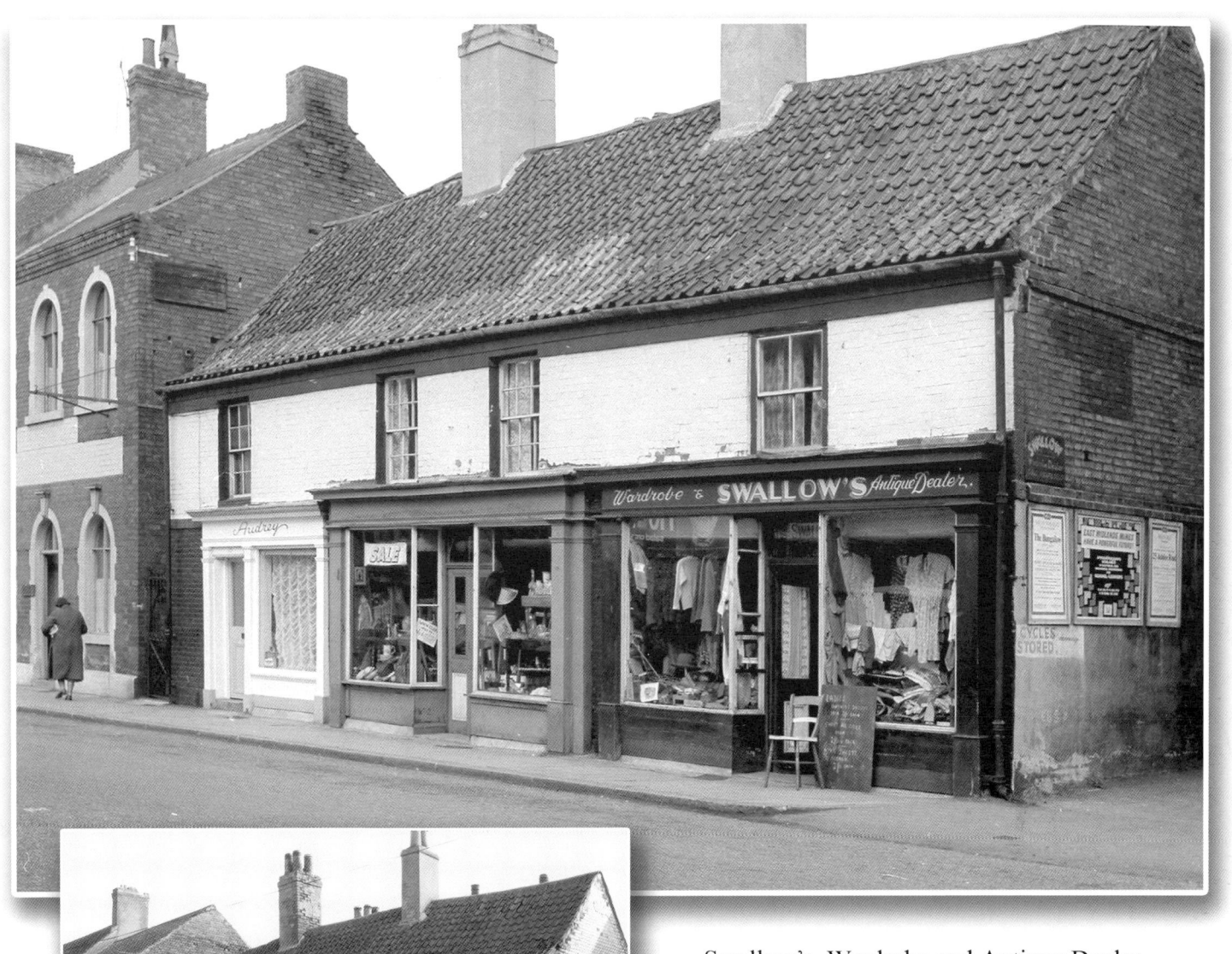

Swallow's, Wardrobe and Antique Dealer

Annie Swallow sold almost everything, if she hadn't got it, she could no doubt get it. The board outside advertises ladies skirts from 2/- (10p) and gents shirts at 2/6 (13p).
Cycles could be stored for the day down the side passage for only a shilling (5p)
The poster on the wall proclaims that "East Midland Mines have a powerful future". Margaret Thatcher was but a humble greengrocer's daughter when this photo was taken.

Churchgate, The Portland Arms

Named after one of the Dukes who owned nearly everything around here at one time. Burtons the butchers and Fred Akers the bookie were on one side, on the other was Franklin's shop, officially numbers one and two Moorgate and now under the relief road junction.

76

Moorgate, The East Midland Bus Depot

The bus depot remained derelict for many years until the Focus DIY store was built. Most of the houses here were demolished long before to make way for the relief road.

77

Moorgate, Tim Taylor's Banana Warehouse

Sad to note that the derelict property remaining was the only one with the preservation order on it!
The shop on Wellington Street end became the Coin-Op washeteria before becoming a fine apartment block with some quite interesting architectural features.
Williamson's Shell garage site is now a large filling station and carwash.

Moorgate, Waterfield's Offices

These properties were last used as offices for the tannery behind them, now a housing estate.
Yes, the pictures are the right way round! The buildings are at last being renovated and should be much improved shortly.

Moorgate, Waterfield's House

Originally the tannery owners house, this property served as a canteen for the workforce before demolition in the 60's to allow a new access road for the expanding factory. Waterfield's tannery is best remembered for the smell which permeated the town when the wind happened to be in the wrong direction. Further expansion took place in the 70's, but the whole factory site is now a housing estate.

Moorgate, The Queen's Head Inn

Originally the inside was a number of small rooms, the removal of a few walls has created a pleasant restaurant.

81

The Queens Head Inn, Moorgate.

The properties from the public house to Water Lane were demolished to make way for the filling station.
It has been suggested that the original house builder's plan may have been to have the houses going around the corner into Water Lane. Why else would he build extra chimneys' on the end houses when there were only fireplaces in the downstairs front room and the upstairs front bedroom?

Moorgate, Water Lane

Water Lane leads down to the River Idle and was once the site of a brick and tile works and football ground of the same name. All have long since disappeared under a housing development and the lane itself has been realigned closer to the side of The Brick and Tile Public House.
The chimney and buildings visible in the distace belong to the Clarks Dyeworks on Hallcroft Road.

83

Moorgate, Chapel's Lane

I dont think that is the official title, but many people have told me that name. The Bethel Chapel is at the bottom of the lane, but the chapel like building on the right is actually the Saint Saviour's mission room, currently used as a rehearsal room.

Moorgate, The Bethel Chapel, off Bank Terrace.

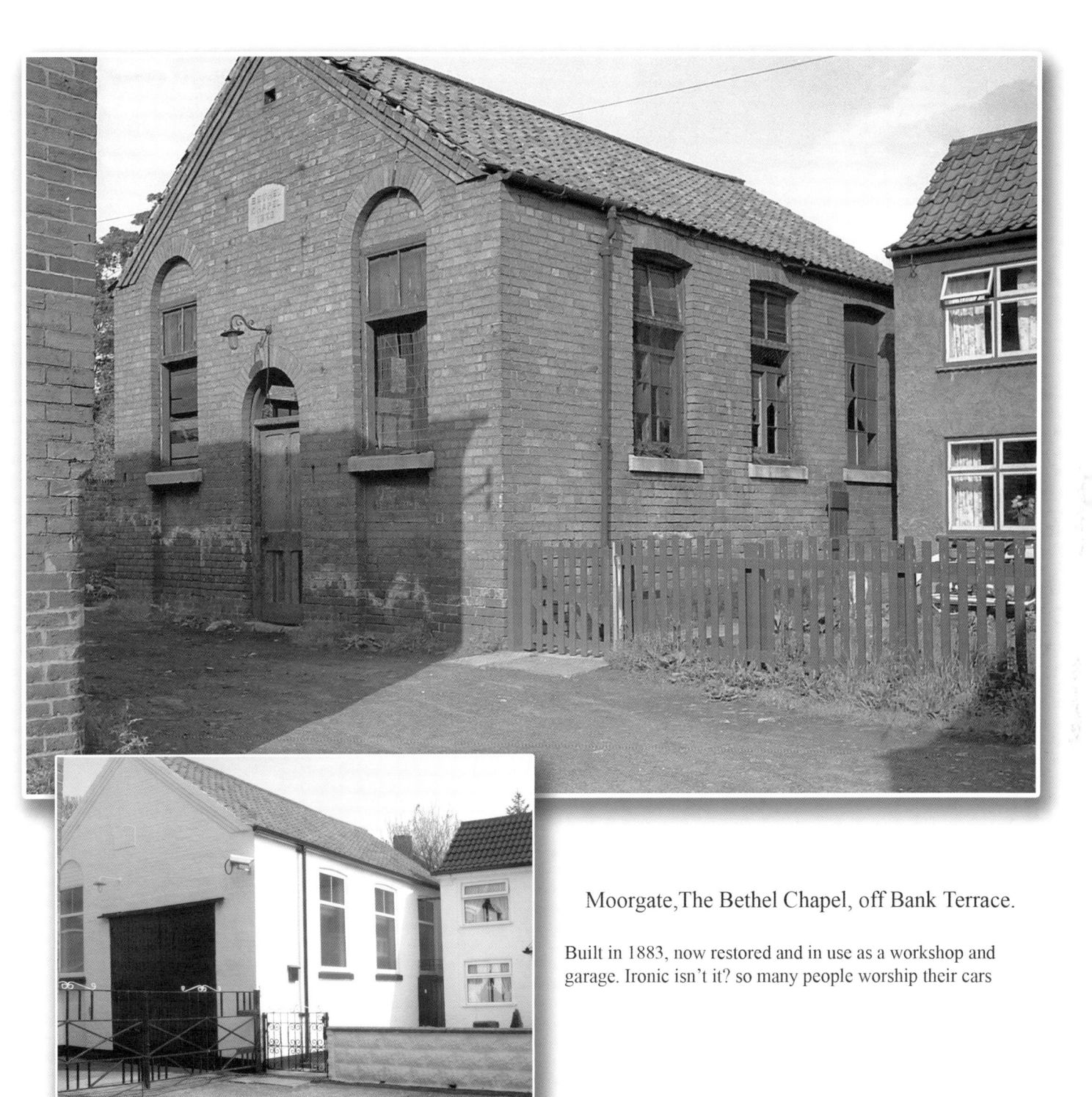

Built in 1883, now restored and in use as a workshop and garage. Ironic isn't it? so many people worship their cars

Moorgate, Bank Terrace

A shortcut from Moorgate through to Wellington Street. The cottages were demolished as far as window level and the remaining wall used as a support for the banking that the new houses are built upon. The bricked in doors are still visible.

Moorgate, The Brick and Tile Public House

Now standing alone, once in a row of shops and houses. On one side now is the realigned Water Lane, on the other is the inevitable car park.

Moorgate, The Brick and Tile Public House

Reputedly named after the brickyard down Water Lane. Products from the brickyard went by boat down the river Idle, bypassing Bolham Mill by way of the lock provided by Retford Corporation. Only small vessels could be used because of the difficulty of navigating the winding river further downstream.
The football pitch at the rear of the pub is now a housing estate of senior citizen's dwellings.

Bolham Lane, The Cottage

This little cottage, halfway down Bolham Lane, may have looked picturesque. I was informed that when it rained heavily, water from the fields behind came in the back door and went out the front. The occupants simply moved upstairs.
Bricks and windows and roofing tiles have been recycled to make a superior garden shed.

Bolham Lane, The Mill Worker's Cottages

Nothing remains of this row of cottages today.
 A modern property stands on the site, but does not enjoy the same view over open pastures that these houses did.
 The River Idle has been "canalised" to help prevent flooding, whilst the fields were first quarried, then redeveloped into fishing lakes with mobile homes dotted around the site.

The Mill Manager's House, Bolham Lane.

Bolham Mill tailrace, in the forground, was removed when the river was deepened to alleviate flooding some years ago.
The site of the mill is now a residential home.
The sandstone caves probably housed some of Retford's first residents and were in use for storage until quite recently.
The Manager's house was demolished in the 1960's

Hallcroft Road, Clarks Dyeworks.

Once one of the town's largest employers and longest established business'. The dyeworks were originally located on what is now Chapelgate car park, a section of which is named Dyer's Court.
Goodwin's fish and chip remains, but is under new ownership and now opens for breakfasts.

Bridgegate, Hospital Road, Sneath's Corner

One of the town's pioneer motor traders back in the 1920's. Descendant Cyril Sneath was the first Retford garage owner to introduce Japanese vehicles when he became a Toyota Agent in the 1960's, much to the disgust of the other British car dealerships in the town.

93

Clarks Garage, Bridgegate.

The petrol pumps were actually located through the archway, inside the building. When the house was demolished the pumps were moved to the yard outside. After filling up, cars were then rotated on a turntable so that they could exit onto the main road in a forward direction.

As well as a Roote's Group car dealership, the business also incorporated Clark's Tyres and Clark's Auto Electrical. UltraMarine operated a boat business here for a number of years after Charlie Clark and Son closed down.

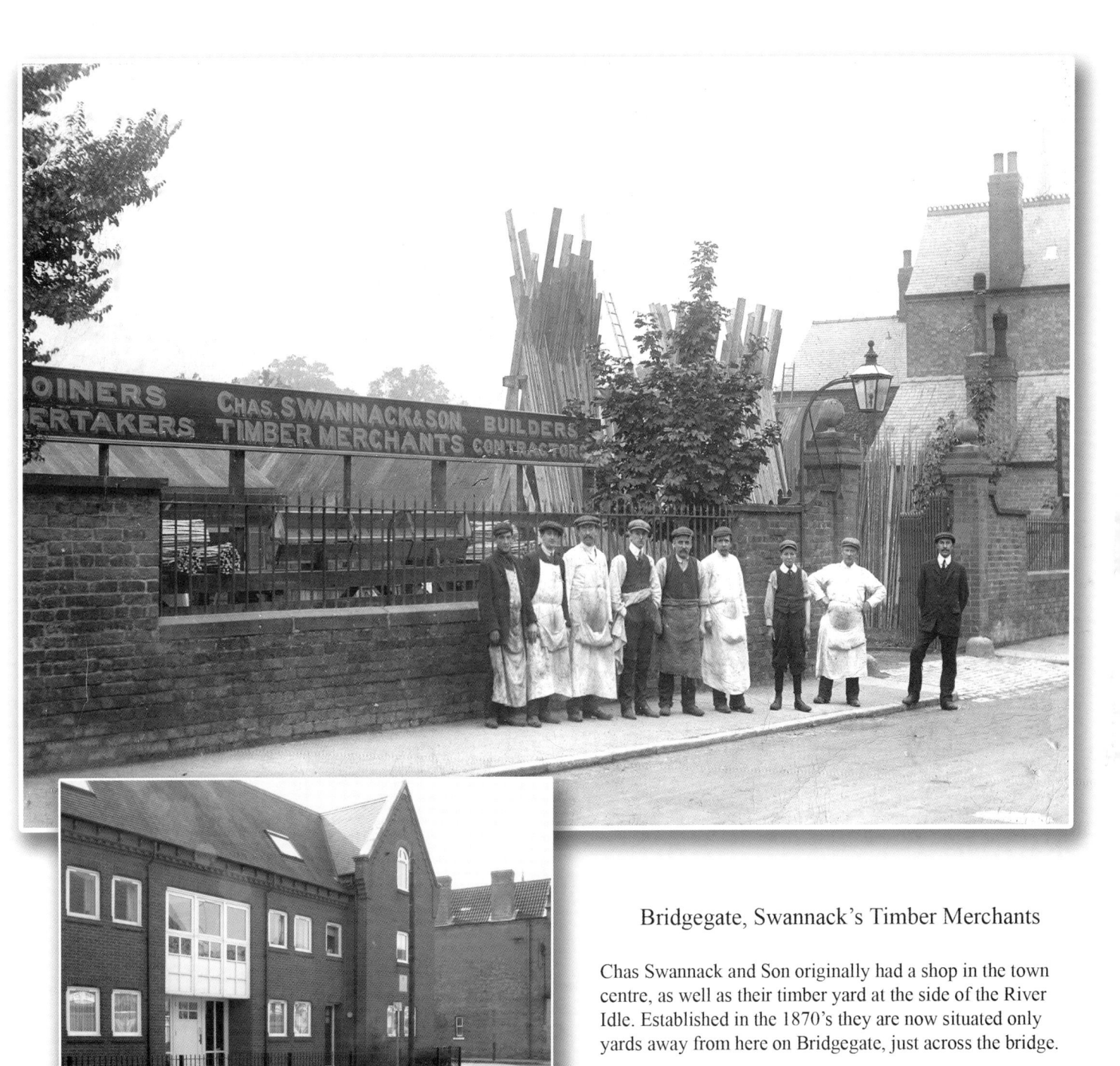

Bridgegate, Swannack's Timber Merchants

Chas Swannack and Son originally had a shop in the town centre, as well as their timber yard at the side of the River Idle. Established in the 1870's they are now situated only yards away from here on Bridgegate, just across the bridge.

95

Bridgegate, West's Gun Shop

The bracket that supported the gun shop sign still remains on K & H sports, almost 70 years after this shot was taken.
When Butler's shop was demolished in the 60's for an access to the new supermarket (now Argos) the Chinese restaurant next door collapsed.

The Market Square and Cenotaph

Back to where we started on the market square and not a car to be seen, just empty parking spaces.
I hope we've brought back a few memories, or possibly shown you the Retford I still fondly remember.

If you've enjoyed looking at

RETFORD OLD AND NEW

take a look at

WWW.REDI-IMAGE.COM

If you have any old photographs of
Retford and the surrounding villages that
you would like to share with others
please contact us for further details.

Tel: 07092 804433
Fax: 07092 804434
info@redi-image.com